The Meteorologist In Me

By Brittney Shipp
Illustrated by Robin Boyer

The Meteorologist In Me
ISBN: 978-0-692-75798-7 (paperback)
Copyright © 2016 by Brittney Shipp
THE POWER OF LOVE BOOKS, Publisher

"Summmmmmer, Summer... Time to come inside..."

"...Dinner is ready, come set the table," yelled Mama Winters from the kitchen window.

"How was your day Summer, Sunny, Storm, and Sky?"
asked Papa Winters.
"GREAT!" shouts Summer's brother, Sunny.

Summer hushes her brothers, "Shhh...the weather is on...This is *my* favorite part of the news!! I think *I* could do that one day." Summer *nervously* utters.

"HA HA HA!!! Yeah right. We love you Summer, but you don't know enough about the weather to be a weather woman" says Storm, Summer's oldest brother.

7

" I know why!! It's because it's *too* warm in the city for snow."
Summer replies to her brother, with a little attitude.

April Showers: The temperatures in the city will stay ABOVE 32 degrees. At 32 degrees, water freezes!

Weather FACT!
Water FREEZES at 32 degrees.

32°F

"That was just a lucky guess!" exclaimed Sky,
Summer's youngest brother with a smile.

"Alright you guys...That's enough...Time to get ready for bed so you are all rested for school tomorrow. Everyone remember, you can do anything you put your mind to! Don't let anyone tell you otherwise" added Mama Winters.

Summer thinks to herself...*It wasn't a lucky guess. I like to read every night about the snow, hurricanes, tornadoes and more! Maybe I could be a meteorologist just like April Showers...I just have to BELIEVE in myself! No matter what!*

At school the next day, the teacher says, "I have a *special* announcement!
We are heading to the mountains to see the SNOW!"
"AWESOME!!" yell all the kids in the classroom.

"I just love the snow!" Summer exclaims to her best friend, Monsoon. "Did you know that if you look at a snowflake up close under a microscope, you would see that it has six arms that stick out?"

"WOW! That's SO COOL! Sounds like you love weather." says Monsoon.

Weather FACT!

A snowflake has 6 arms

Summer continues, "Yep, I want to tell people all about the weather on TV one day!"

"Oh Summer! You are *too shy* for that. I think that would be *too hard* for you," Monsoon playfully replies with a laugh.

Summer softly says, "Maybe you're right."

When Summer gets home, she thinks to herself, *"I know I have a dream, but it's hard to BELIEVE in myself if I keep hearing I can't do it. For now, I will keep studying."*

14

"That's right, everyone remember, you can do anything you put your mind to. Don't let anyone tell you otherwise." added Mama Winters with a smile.

the end.

This book belongs to:

_____

Career Day!

Cloud types:

Cumulus   Stratus   Cirrus

"Attention students, as you know, it's Career Day and I have arranged a special guest for you all." said Mr. Rains. Summer recognizes her immediately but sits quietly with a big smile on her face.

Weather FACT!

3 main types of clouds:

Cumulus

Stratus

Cirrus

15

"Hello Everyone, my name is April Showers and I'm a meteorologist. Does anyone know what a meteorologist does?"

me·te·or·ol·o·gist

a person that studies the atmosphere and forecasts the weather

Do you study meteors?

Are you a scientist?

Career Day!

About the Author:

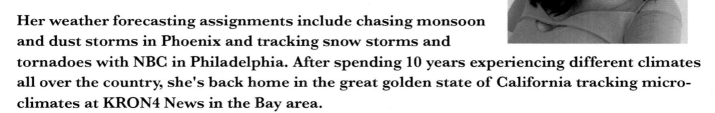

Brittney Shipp is a nationally recognized, Emmy-nominated TV Meteorologist from Los Angeles, California. Shipp earned an undergraduate degree from UCLA and Certificate of Broadcast Meteorology from Mississippi State University. She's appeared nationally on MSNBC's Early Today, First Look and Morning Joe.

Her weather forecasting assignments include chasing monsoon and dust storms in Phoenix and tracking snow storms and tornadoes with NBC in Philadelphia. After spending 10 years experiencing different climates all over the country, she's back home in the great golden state of California tracking micro-climates at KRON4 News in the Bay area.

Brittney Shipp has always enjoyed reading to young students in classrooms. After a few frustrating trips to the book store, she decided to author her first children's book.

It's her dream to energize young women and all students to choose weather and science-related careers. She hopes *The Meteorologist in Me* encourages everyone to take a step forward towards making their dreams a reality.

HELP US SPREAD THE WORD!
Take a Picture with our Book & Tag Us!

 @Meteorologistinme

 @Meteorologistinme

 @Brittneyshipp

GIVE THE GIFT OF OUR BOOKS!
www.thepoweroflovebooks.com

Dedicated to:
My loving and supportive parents- Deborah and Joe Shipp.
Thank you for empowering a little girl to pursue a big dream. –BS

To my parents for their unwavering support of all
my dreams and aspirations, big and small. –RB

Summer shouts out, "You study the weather every day!"
"How did you know that?" says April Showers with amazement.

17

Summer shyly tells the whole class her dream, "That's what I want to be."

"You *can't* be on TV, HA HA HA! You'll get *too* nervous!" scream all the students in a burst of laughter.

"Thank you for joining us, Ms. April Showers," says the teacher, Mr. Rains.
Then Mr. Rains smiles when he notices April Showers and Summer still chatting.

Back at the Winters' home, Mama Winters calls out of the kitchen window,
"Come on inside boys...time for dinner and set the table."

"Where's Summer? She's going to miss her favorite part-THE WEATHER!
HA HA HA!" asks all the Winters brothers. Still poking fun at Summer,
they head inside for dinner and to watch the evening news.

April Showers: Tonight we have a SPECIAL weather guest helping with the forecast. If she keeps studying, she'll become a future TV meteorologist! Welcome, Summer Winters.

Mama Winters smiles and all her brothers shout, "WOW!!! Look at Summer! She's on TV talking about the weather!"
"Well, we always knew she *could* do it. I told you she would be GREAT!" Sky says to Storm and Sunny.